LIFE BEYON

Reflections on Dying and Afterlife

John C. Tormey

238
TO

LIGUORI
PUBLICATIONS

One Liguori Drive
Liguori, Missouri 63057
(314) 464-2500

Imprimi Potest:
John F. Dowd, C.SS.R.
Provincial, St. Louis Province
Redemptorist Fathers

Imprimatur:
+ John N. Wurm, Ph.D., S.T.D.
Vicar General, Archdiocese of St. Louis

The Imprimi Potest and the Imprimatur are a declaration that a book or pamphlet is considered to be free from doctrinal or moral error. It is not implied that those who have granted the Imprimi Potest and Imprimatur agree with the contents, opinions or statements expressed.

ISBN 0-89243-151-2

Quotes by Viktor Frankl taken from *Man's Search for Meaning: An Introduction to Logotherapy,* copyright © 1959, Beacon Press, 25 Beacon Street, Boston, Massachusetts 02108. Used by permission.

All Scripture quotes are taken from the *Revised Standard Version Common Bible,* copyrighted © 1973. Used by permission.

Cover Design: Pam Hummelsheim

Cover Photo: Frank Bez

I dedicate these reflections
to my dad
who made his passage to perfection
on April 26, 1979,
the day of his
thirty-eighth wedding anniversary.

CONTENTS

To the Reader from the Author

I enjoyed a warm and affectionate conversation with my mom and dad the evening of April 25, 1979. We talked about their thirty-eighth wedding anniversary which we would be celebrating the next evening.

Jeannie and I had been married only a short time, and I was absorbing all the love my parents felt for each other as I squeezed Jeannie's hand. The four of us talked about the old house Jeannie and I had just bought. We welcomed my parents over to see it after the closing which was only two days away.

All our plans were made. I left my parents that evening with a kiss and a hug. My mind was bursting with dreams. Life seemed to be going so smoothly. I went to sleep that night with great expectations for the next day.

The next morning the telephone rang at 7:30. I will never forget what my mom said. "Johnny, I can't wake Dad up. I think he is dead."

My dad meant everything to me. The shock and pain that came with the news of his death ripped me apart. It was the greatest emotional suffering of my life.

I drove to my parents' house, telling myself that this was not really happening. It was Dad's wedding anniversary. He was so happy and healthy. And we had plans for Friday. I was numb and I was angry. The car was not going fast enough and I felt totally powerless.

When I arrived and saw Dad so lifeless in his bed, my heart seemed to break into pieces. I hugged and kissed him with words of love and gratitude. All the ideas I had expressed so often in the courses on death and dying that I teach suddenly became my own feelings. I had just shared a reflection by Richard Bach with my students that week: "You teach best what you most want to learn yourself." For the first time, I was learning what I was teaching.

My dad's death initiated one of the most difficult times of my life. But the caring of Jeannie, my family, my friends — and the valuable library of reflections I had collected from reading — gradually helped to heal the pain of loss and separation.

The Book of Proverbs tells us: "Sickness, the spirit of a person can endure but when the spirit is broken, who can bear this?" When the spirit leaves the body of a person we love, we say that the person "ex-spires." That is, the spirit goes out of the person. For those who share love and friendship, that process leaves an agonizing void which we call grief. The process can also affect your own spirit just as my dad's ex-spiring affected me on April 26, 1979.

When a person's spirit is broken, it needs inspiration to fill the void. That is the purpose of this booklet. The inspirational reflections you find here will not prevent the grief and bereavement you experience. But these reflections can help to strengthen you as time, good friends, and your personal fortitude mend your broken spirit.

The reflections in this booklet do not guarantee immediate relief. What they offer is light during a time when darkness makes it difficult to find a direction into the future. As John Dunne says in his book *The Other Side of Earth:* "Illumination of the mind occurs not so much through the acquisition of new information as through the discovery of a new standpoint from which the available information can be regarded."

John C. Tormey

1. A Time for Everything

For everything there is a season,
  and a time for every matter under heaven:
a time to be born, and a time to die;
a time to plant, and a time to pluck up what is planted;
a time to kill, and a time to heal;
a time to break down, and a time to build up;
a time to weep, and a time to laugh;
a time to mourn, and a time to dance;
a time to cast away stones, and a time to gather
  stones together;
a time to embrace, and a time to refrain from embracing;
a time to seek, and a time to lose;
a time to keep, and a time to cast away;
a time to rend, and a time to sew;
a time to keep silence, and a time to speak;
a time to love, and a time to hate;
a time for war, and a time for peace.

Ecclesiastes 3:1-8

Seeing God

For now we see in a mirror dimly, but then face to face. Now I know in part; then I shall understand fully, even as I have been fully understood.

1 Corinthians 13:12

Early one morning in winter I was getting ready to go to work. As I stood in front of the mirror shaving, the lights went off. I kept on shaving in the dark, which resulted in several painful nicks. In a few minutes the lights came back on. I then discovered whole areas of my face still unshaven, as well as the razor nicks I had made in the dark.

The experience of death is like seeing the lights come on. We find out what we missed and why we suffered.

Sometimes it is frustrating to realize that God knows all about me but that I know so little about him. Getting to know a human person is a happy experience. What an ecstatic experience it must be to know God as he really is.

The LORD is my light and my salvation;
. . . I believe that I shall see the goodness of the LORD in the land of the living! (Psalm 27:1,13)

Transformation

Lo! I tell you a mystery. We shall not all sleep, but we shall all be changed . . . For this perishable nature must put on the imperishable, and this mortal nature must put on immortality.

1 Corinthians 15:51,53

Death is best defined as transformation. Life continues in a new form, with a new beginning and a new freedom. As the survivors bid farewell, the deceased is saying hello to a new life.

The caterpillar who becomes the butterfly is an example of this transformation. The crawling caterpillar evolves into a gliding butterfly — a creature of beauty and freedom. The same process takes place in the death experience. Life is transformed, not ended.

God is the great Transformer. He transforms parts of his earthly creation into human form. He transforms the dead trees of winter into the budding trees of spring. God has an excellent record. You can trust him completely. At death he will transform you into a person radiant with life, beauty, and freedom.

"O death, where is thy victory?
O death, where is thy sting?"
(1 Corinthians 15:55)

The Spirit Within

If the Spirit of him who raised Jesus from the dead dwells in you, he who raised Christ Jesus from the dead will give life to your mortal bodies also through his Spirit which dwells in you.

Romans 8:11

The United States space shuttle *Columbia* is a marvel of human ingenuity. *Columbia* leaves its launching pad with the help of two rockets which are discarded after lift-off. Though short-lived, the rockets give the spacecraft direction and propulsion, freeing it from the earth's atmosphere.

Human existence is somewhat like those rockets. It launches the human spirit into the life of eternity.

Human existence is merely one phase of our life. It has a short-lived but important purpose: the preparation and eventual lifting of our spirit into the freedom we call afterlife.

When *Columbia's* rockets detach from the spacecraft and fall back to earth, *Columbia* soars onward, freed of their weight. When your body dies, your spirit soars to God, carried by his Spirit dwelling in you.

To thee, O LORD, I lift up my soul.
Relieve the troubles of my heart,
*   and bring me out of my distresses*
(Psalm 25:1,17).

God's Time

Space provides room for being and time provides room for becoming. Space is the vehicle of determination and being, and time is the vehicle of freedom and value. A person's existence and the gift of time may be viewed as permission to partake in the creativity of the world.

Samuel Alexander

The ancient Greeks employed two words for time: *chronos* and *kairos*. *Chronos* means "clock" time — the measured time of hours, days, and years. Hence, the English word *chronology*. In contrast, the Greeks used the word *kairos*, meaning God's time or "eternal" time.

God's time does not always blend in with clock time. So it is that people die on Christmas Day, on birthdays and anniversaries, or on the day of their retirement. The calendar leaves us feeling cheated and angry. Couldn't God have waited until the man's daughter was married or for a few good years of retirement or at least until after the Christmas holidays?

Death is the call of the *kairos*, a beckoning to enter a time zone which is forever and eternal. A person who dies does not "run out of time." He simply enters God's *kairos* eternity which has no clocks and calendars, no more deadlines or accountings.

Jesus Christ is the same yesterday
and today and for ever (Hebrews 13:8).

Servants, Not Masters

None of us lives to himself, and none of us dies to himself.
If we live, we live to the Lord, and if we die, we die to the
Lord; so then whether we live or whether we die, we are the
Lord's. For to this end Christ died and lived again, that he
might be Lord both of the dead and of the living.

Romans 14:7-9

The existence of insurance companies is mute testimony
to the fact that we are not masters of our destiny. This life
has been loaned to us. It can be called to accountability in
a split second. The tomb is a sobering reminder that we are
God's servants.

Once we realize that we are not masters of our destiny,
we begin to seek our strength and sustenance in God. It is
then that life becomes so much more pleasant and mean-
ingful. With that attitude, we are less inclined to become
angry and depressed when life is recalled in the dying and
death process. Instead of becoming frustrated with the life
we will not have in the future, we are able to enjoy with
gratitude the life we still have.

O Lord, help me to remember that
nothing is going to happen to me today
that you and I together cannot handle.
(Contemporary Prayer)

Until We Meet Again

May the Lord watch between me and thee
While we are absent one from the other.

Mizpah Benediction

Medals with this beautiful blessing inscribed on them have been struck in silver, gold, and pewter. One person takes half of the medal and the other person keeps the other half. Their farewell is filled with the fond hope of bringing the two halves together at some future time.

The Mizpah blessing is very appropriate for the separation of persons called death, because their reunion is bound to happen. Rather than "good-bye," it is far more accurate a reality to say "until we meet again."

For the living, the separation called death seems so final and initially unbearable. Some people seem to die "of a broken heart" soon after a loved one has passed on. But the living can cherish the fond hope of a reunion because death offers the same passage to us all. In the meantime of your waiting, as the calendar years pass by, the deceased does not forget you. The Mizpah of your lives will become one again.

May the Lord watch between me and thee
While we are absent one from the other.
(Mizpah Benediction)

God's Personal Touch

"Let not your hearts be troubled; believe in God, believe also in me. In my Father's house are many rooms; if it were not so, would I have told you that I go to prepare a place for you? And when I go and prepare a place for you, I will come again and will take you to myself, that where I am you may be also. And you know the way where I am going."

John 14:1-4

Jesus shared this promise with his disciples just before his death. Jesus urges us not to be worried and upset when we think about our own death. The separation is only temporary and there is plenty of room for us all to enjoy the love and mercy of his Father.

Jesus has assured us that death is the loving touch of his embrace. Death is an experience which Jesus himself handles personally. It is the time for going back home where our spirit first came from. As Mother Teresa of Calcutta says: "To return to God is to return home."

Jesus promised that he would not tell us this if it were not so. Saint John had seen Jesus after his Resurrection. John was convinced of the promise because he was convinced that Jesus is one with his Father and that "nothing is impossible with God."

One thing have I asked of the LORD,
that will I seek after;
that I may dwell in the house of the LORD
all the days of my life . . . (Psalm 27:4).

The Image of God

*So God created man in his own image, in the image of God
he created him; male and female he created them.*

Genesis 1:27

In human civilization there are two general views of
what is valuable about a human person. One of the two
views puts emphasis on the body. An example of this emphasis is the cult of physical beauty and stylish clothing.

The other view of what is valuable about persons lays
emphasis on the spirit, the human soul. This emphasis has
endured more strongly in Oriental cultures.

Regardless of age, sex, religion, race, or social standing,
every human person is a living image of the Creator. This
image, rooted in the spirit, is what makes you and every
other human being equal in the presence of God.

When we stand in the light of God at the moment of
death, what matters to us is not wealth or success. What
matters to us then is how we revered God's image, how we
respected and loved ourselves and others.

O LORD, thou hast searched me and known me!
Thou knowest when I sit down and when I rise up;
thou discernest my thought from afar.
Thou searchest out my path and my lying down,
*   and art acquainted with all my ways.*
(Psalm 139:1-3)

God's Embrace

Beloved, we are God's children now; it does not yet appear what we shall be, but we know that when he appears we shall be like him, for we shall see him as he is.

1 John 3:2

Modern science describes death as cardiac and respiratory arrest or the cessation of brain activity. Looking beyond this impersonal data, Christians can describe death as the embrace of Jesus. Death is not merely something that happens to us; it is a meeting with Someone we love. The instant of death is a warm, joyful embrace with Divinity.

When Jesus appears to us, Saint John reveals, the sight of him will transform our entire being. If we survivors could glimpse the deceased in the rapture of their new life, our hearts would rip with joy rather than pain.

"My soul magnifies the Lord,
and my spirit rejoices in God my Savior,
for he has regarded the low estate of his handmaiden.
For behold, henceforth all generations
*   will call me blessed . . ." (Luke 1:46-48).*

God's Plan for You

To them God chose to make known how great among the Gentiles are the riches of the glory of this mystery, which is Christ in you, the hope of glory.

Colossians 1:27

God has a plan for you. You may not grasp God's plan as you go through the stages of your life. But you have this assurance: at the end of your journey you will share "the glory of this mystery" because "Christ in you" is guiding and directing you.

God's plan for you follows the stages of Jesus' passage from death to life. If Jesus died and rose from the dead, so will you. His Easter dawn is the promise that God is your inheritance.

When you accept Jesus as your Lord and Savior, you can surrender all your fears and anxieties. Jesus is the Guide who has passed through the whole process of dying to the glory of new life. He will personally take you through the whole passage, so that like him, you can say to the Father:

I glorified thee on earth, having accomplished the work which thou gavest me to do; and now, Father, glorify thou me in thy own presence . . . (John 17:4-5).

Resurrection

"I am the resurrection and the life; he who believes in me, though he die, yet shall he live, and whoever lives and believes in me shall never die."

John 11:25-26

At the heart of our Christian concept of death and afterlife is the belief in Jesus' Resurrection.

After Jesus rose, he appeared to his disciples who were in hiding. Thomas, one of the twelve, was not present. When the others told him they had seen Jesus risen, Thomas refused to accept their word. Eight days later, Jesus appeared again and Thomas was there. After Thomas touched his wounds, Jesus said to him: "Blessed are those who have not seen and yet believe" (John 20:29).

Faith in Jesus' promise means trusting Jesus completely. It means taking him at his word, even though we cannot see or touch the wounds in his risen body. This deep person-to-person faith takes courage. As Soren Kierkegaard, the Christian existentialist, wrote: "Real faith requires a risk which is created only from a tremendous act of courage."

Faith in Jesus' promise passes beyond human science to the Person himself. When our trust in him becomes mature, we know that he will raise us from death as surely as he raised his dear friend Lazarus. We are able to say with Saint Paul: "O death, where is thy victory? O death, where is thy sting?" (1 Corinthians 15:55)

I wait for the LORD, my soul waits,
and in his word I hope . . . (Psalm 130:5).

2. The God of Life

It is the spirit that gives life,
the flesh is of no avail . . . .
And this is eternal life,
that they know thee the only true God,
and Jesus Christ whom thou hast sent.

John 6:63, 17:3

Beyond Atheism

For all men who were ignorant of God were foolish by nature; and they were unable from the good things that are seen to know him who exists, nor did they recognize the craftsman while paying heed to his works . . . let them know how much better than these is their Lord, for the author of beauty created them.

Wisdom 13:1,3

The existentialist philosopher Albert Camus once reflected: "Believing in God amounts to coming to terms with death. When you have accepted death, the problem of God will be solved."

For Christians, Camus' insight works in reverse. It is when we surrender to God that the problem of death is solved.

The atheist sees God as "the problem." To the atheist, the "good things" we experience in life do not point beyond themselves to "their author." To atheistic eyes, this world is a bleak, closed system that has no rhyme or reason, no Beyond.

People with this outlook grasp at every straw to cheat or subdue death. They try to reduce death to a merely physical reality when it is basically much more — a spiritual experience.

"Worthy art thou, our Lord and God, to receive glory and honor and power, for thou didst create all things, and by thy will they existed and were created" (Revelation 4:11).

The "More" That We Seek

We dream, fight and work to gain a position, a bank account, a title, a discovery, and while we are still savoring our triumph it begins to lose its taste, to shrivel and fade away.

God is behind every voice of disillusionment that cries: You want something that will always be different and new, that will never leave you feeling small and inadequate.

Juan Arias

God can be discovered in the beauty and goodness of creation. God can also be glimpsed behind the disillusionment that follows in the wake of material satisfactions. As Saint Augustine said, "Our hearts are restless, God, until they rest in you."

The body can be satisfied with pleasure temporarily, but the spirit still groans for that something more which human existence simply cannot provide. The emptiness, the craving we sense in ourselves, is our doorway to God, the only Source of true satisfaction.

My soul thirsts for God, for the living God.
When shall I come and behold the face of God?
(Psalm 42:2)

Converging on God

Nature is the base of something and this something is the figure of Someone who is hidden. . . . The ultimate explanation of life's movement is that the universe is converging upon God.

Teilhard de Chardin

If the universe were not moving in an ordered and rhythmic way, our world would be a nightmare of chaos. In fact, our world is not in chaos. God has set the rhythm of the universe and we share in the harmony of his plan.

Teilhard de Chardin saw all creation as a constant, rhythmic flow to and from a central, ultimate Source whom we call God. When we are born we become part of that Divine Milieu. When we die we bring the universe a degree closer to converging upon God.

Gabriel Marcel called the human person *homo viator* — the person on a journey, the person who is constantly "becoming." On the path of becoming, pain and death accompany our growth to higher stages of life. In those moments of pain, we are not alone. The Lord is with us, bringing all creation to himself.

Our Father who art in heaven,
Hallowed be thy name.
Thy kingdom come,
Thy will be done,
   On earth as it is in heaven. (Matthew 6:9-10)

What Heaven Is Like

*Ever since the creation of the world his invisible nature,
namely, his eternal power and deity, has been clearly
perceived in the things that have been made.*

Romans 1:20

When you gaze into the starry vastness of the night sky
or watch a shimmering sunrise on the water, you are looking at a reflection of God. And when you experience the
fullness of loving and being loved, what you experience is
a foretaste of heaven — the God who is Love.

Heaven is a place where we experience perfect super-
natural bliss. It is not the pleasure that comes from posses-
sions and bodily sensations, but the happiness of awakening to God in all his fullness.

Heaven is life without the chaos of hate, dishonesty,
greed, and jealousy. If we could deepen our experience of
love, of God, to an infinite degree, we could then begin to
imagine what heaven is like.

*Thou hast multiplied, O Lord my God,
    thy wondrous deeds and thy thoughts toward us;
    none can compare with thee! (Psalm 40:5)*

God's Promise

". . . no eye has seen, nor ear heard, nor the heart of man conceived, what God has prepared for those who love him."

1 Corinthians 2:9

The pain of losing a loved one is experienced only by survivors. The deceased are experiencing ineffable joy that no human eye has yet seen or human emotion yet felt.

No matter how far we stretch our imagination, we still fall short of picturing the glorious surprise that awaits us.

Meanwhile, on this earth, God's kingdom is already present in mystery. When the Lord returns, it will be brought into full flower.

At the end of time, Jesus will "make all things new" (Revelation 21:5). "He will wipe away every tear from their eyes, and death shall be no more" (Revelation 21:4).

Surrender yourself to God's promise. Take him at his word. What God has in store for those who love him is nothing less than himself.

O LORD . . . Such knowledge is too wonderful
  for me; it is high,
I cannot attain it (Psalm 139:1,6).

Love Does Not Die

God is love, and he who abides in love abides in God, and God abides in Him.

1 John 4:16

Feel loved by those who have passed directly into God's presence. Enjoy the guarantee that you will be reunited with them in love.

Love transcends earthly experience because it is not only human but divine. Unlike pleasurable experiences that depend on the senses, love does not die.

Love is basically a spiritual experience that comes in many forms. We love as spouses, fathers, mothers, sons, daughters, friends. Underlying each of these relationships is the caring of one person's spirit for another.

In this life we express our caring in visible ways. But our caring lives on after the visible expressions are no more.

When you die and are reunited with the people you love, you will realize that genuine love never dies.

For the LORD is good; his steadfast love endures for ever (Psalm 100:5).

Where Is God?

"The kingdom of God is not coming with signs to be observed; nor will they say, 'Lo, here it is!' or 'There!' for behold, the kingdom of God is in the midst of you."

Luke 17:20-21

Death has been misconceived as a journey to a God who is millions of light years beyond the galaxies of endless space. The truth is, the kingdom of God is not "out there" somewhere. It is, as Jesus told us, right here in our midst.

Saint Augustine remarked that God is more deeply present to us than we are to ourselves. So going to God is not a matter of traveling like an astronaut in outer space. It is a matter of discovering ourselves in his presence.

The theologian Paul Tillich spoke of God as "the ground of our being." Every moment of our existence flows from God's presence to us. Saint Paul referred to this all-enveloping presence of God when he quoted a Greek poet who said, "In him we live and move and have our being" (Acts 17:28).

Like the sponge that lives in the depths of the ocean, we live in God. When we pass from this earthly way of being, we find ourselves where we always have been — in the embrace of God. So no one ever dies alone. And no one "travels" to God. He is here in our midst.

He is before all things, and in him all things hold together (Colossians 1:17).

Beyond Expression

Flesh and blood cannot inherit the kingdom of God, nor does the perishable inherit the imperishable.

1 Corinthians 15:50

In his book *Life After Life,* Dr. Raymond Moody records the experiences of near-death patients who have returned from a glimpse of the afterlife. Dr. Moody summarizes his findings with this statement: "The persons involved uniformly characterize their experience as ineffable, that is, inexpressible."

The afterlife experience is humanly inexpressible because it defies the language of space and time. What is mortal cannot describe what is immortal. Yet we continue to frustrate ourselves by seeking space-time definitions of these realities. We will do much better if we give up trying to conquer the beyond and simply give in to its surprise.

Folk humor is filled with stories of Saint Peter at the Pearly Gates. These stories are funny examples of how we project mortal pride and prejudice onto the realm of eternity. They contain the seed of awareness that in the life of the spirit there are no ethnic, racial, or sexual barriers. The more we become aware of this deeper level, the more we can feel at home with the immortal kingdom beyond space and time.

Great is the LORD, and greatly to be praised, and his greatness is unsearchable (Psalm 145:3).

Light in the Darkness

"I am the light of the world; he who follows me will not walk in darkness, but will have the light of life."

John 8:12

In *Life After Life,* Dr. Raymond Moody reports that many people who have experienced near-death say that they came into the presence of a "being of light." Moody writes:

"The light has a very definite personality. The love and warmth which emanate from this being to the dying person are utterly beyond words and he feels completely at ease and accepted in the presence of this being."

Not all who have the near-death experience see this presence of light. But some who have seen it believe that it symbolizes the entrance into a new life.

There is no evidence demanding a Christian or even a religious explanation of this "light" experience. But it is difficult to avoid recalling the parallel that stands out so vividly in the Gospel of John. Throughout that Gospel, Jesus is the Light. In the very first lines of chapter 1, John writes:

In him was life, and the life was the light of men. The light shines in the darkness, and the darkness has not overcome it.

Bless the LORD, O my soul!
O LORD my God, thou art very great!
Thou art clothed with honor and majesty,
*   who coverest thyself with light as*
*   with a garment (Psalm 104:1-2).*

3. The Path to God

For this is why the gospel was preached
even to the dead, that though judged in the flesh
like men, they might live in the spirit like God.

1 Peter 4:6

Why Is There Suffering?

Since therefore Christ suffered in the flesh, arm yourselves with the same thought, for whoever has suffered in the flesh has ceased from sin . . . .

1 Peter 4:1

Why is there suffering? Does it have any redeeming value?

Viktor Frankl suggests: "Suffering ceases to be suffering in some way at the moment it finds a meaning, such as the meaning of a sacrifice." Suffering purifies us in the ever-becoming process of wholeness and perfection.

Jesus tells us: "Blessed are the pure in heart for they shall see God." The word *pure* is a translation of the Greek word *katharos*, from which we get our English word *catharsis*: a cleansing experience. Suffering does just that. It purifies our hearts and prepares us for the presence of God.

There are different degrees of perfection and, therefore, degrees of God's presence. The greater one's purification, the more one can enjoy the fullness of God's presence.

I consider that the sufferings of this
present time are not worth comparing
with the glory that is to be revealed to us.
For the creation waits with eager longing
for the revealing of the sons of God . . .
(Romans 8:18-19).

The Example of Jesus

For to this you have been called, because Christ also suffered for you, leaving you an example, that you should follow in his steps . . . when he suffered, he did not threaten; but he trusted to him who judges justly.
1 Peter 2:21-23

God never promised that life on earth would be filled with happiness. But Jesus became one with us to show that he would not ask us to do anything he would not do himself. He lived like us; he suffered like us; and he died.

It is human to feel cheated, or angry at God, when we seem to have a greater share of suffering than most people. One of the common questions people ask is, "What did I ever do to deserve this?" The question many of us ask has only two words — *"Why me?"*

There are no humanly satisfying answers to such questions. But there is the towering image of the One who trusted God as he "bore our sins in his body on the tree." When we follow his example, we have all the answer we need.

"For who has known the mind of the Lord
so as to instruct him?" (1 Corinthians 2:16)

God Is Preparing Us

. . . we sigh with anxiety; not that we would be unclothed, but that we would be further clothed, so that what is mortal may be swallowed up by life. He who has prepared us for this very thing is God, who has given us the Spirit as a guarantee.

2 Corinthians 5:4-5

The old saying remains true: We all want to go to heaven, but nobody wants to die to get there.

We know that death puts an end to anxiety, depression, and physical suffering. But we also know that dying can be a painful experience emotionally and physically. And we dread the unknown. So most of us cling to this life, seeking all means to prolong it.

God is the one who has prepared us for this change called death. If we let that fact sink in, we can approach our own death with more serenity than dread. Once we accept the inevitable change that God is preparing for us, we can cooperate with his Spirit within us and anticipate death with dignity and hope.

Let us hold fast the confession of our hope without wavering, for he who promised is faithful (Hebrews 10:23).

A Healing Memory

Let the word of Christ dwell in you richly, teach and admonish one another in all wisdom, and sing psalms and hymns and spiritual songs with thankfulness in your hearts to God.

Colossians 3:16

When death occurs, it initiates a process of adjustment: the passage to new life for the deceased and a process of acceptance for the survivors. The funeral or memorial liturgy is an important part of that passage and process.

One of the most healing memories a dying person can give to grieving survivors is his or her personal liturgy. A dying patient's active involvement in the funeral arrangements and liturgy is also good for the patient; it leads to acceptance and consequent peace.

An old Chinese proverb says: "What I hear, I forget. What I see, I remember. What I experience, I understand." Many funeral and memorial liturgies are soon forgotten. But when the dying person puts into words his experience of dying, the liturgy can become a gift of peace, understanding, and even spiritual conversion for those who are present.

Our Savior Christ Jesus . . . abolished death
and brought life and immortality to light
through the gospel (2 Timothy 1:10-11).

Dying with Human Dignity

The dead must be amused when people bewail him, as if to say: It would have been better if you had lived longer and suffered more.

Rabbi Nahman

Medical technology has prolonged human life. But it has also given death a peculiar type of alienation, indignity, and even pain. The tragic fact is: too many people today die in institutions among strangers.

The Hospice movement and other programs are helping dying people and their families to find better options. Families are learning to accept death as a normal part of life. And their loved ones are going through the process of dying with the benefit of family care, familiar surroundings, the least amount of pain, and a great deal of preparation.

We do *not* have to die in an institution among strangers. We *can* choose to prepare for the transition with the same dignity and meaning that characterize other significant events in life.

The choice of a more dignified, natural dying process in a family setting may entail the sacrifice of some extra time on this earth. But as Rabbi Nahman might observe we will be amused in the afterlife when we realize that we now have an eternity of time.

The LORD is my shepherd, I shall not want . . .
though I walk through the valley
*   of the shadow of death, I fear no evil;*
for thou art with me . . . (Psalm 23:1,4).

Focus on the Inner Self

Let not yours be the outward adorning with braiding of hair, decoration of gold, and wearing of fine clothing, but let it be the hidden person of the heart with the imperishable jewel of a gentle and quiet spirit . . .

1 Peter 3:3-4

If you bring your body to a health spa, consider bringing your inner self to the Holy Spirit.

Our bodies were designed with planned obsolescence. Health spas, fine clothes, and jewelry cannot keep these bodies from breaking down. In contrast, our inner self goes on forever.

Western culture is in hot pursuit of the youthful image and physical health. Excellent as these goals may be, the fact is that true, lasting beauty is more than skin-deep. The failure to realize this basic fact has resulted in a whole society that is emotionally unwell.

The best handbook for a healthy spirit is the Scripture. Integrate its precepts into your daily living and you will have both a healthy body and a healthy self.

Come, Holy Spirit,
penetrate the hearts of your faithful
and enkindle in them the fire of your love.
(Prayer to the Holy Spirit)

The Perfection That Is Heaven

You, therefore, must be perfect, as your heavenly
Father is perfect.

Matthew 5:48

A magnificent inspirational resource is the book
Jonathan Livingston Seagull by Richard Bach. The story
of Jonathan's search for perfection is an incentive to seek
the kingdom of heaven which is in our midst (Luke 17:21).

Once we take flight like Jonathan, once "we stop seeing
ourselves as trapped inside a limited body," we then
realize that death is simply a change in life's atmosphere.
We sense that the perfection called heaven is, mysteri-
ously, already within us. As Richard Bach expressed it:
So this is heaven. He saw that his own body was growing bright. The outer form had changed. Heaven is not
a place and it is not a time. Heaven is being perfect.

Blessed be the God and Father of our Lord Jesus Christ,
who has blessed us in Christ with every spiritual blessing
in the heavenly places . . . (Ephesians 1:3).

Take Comfort in Forgiveness

All that the Father gives me will come to me; and him who comes to me I will not cast out . . . . For this is the will of my Father, that every one who sees the Son and believes in him should have eternal life . . . .

John 6:37,40

People who know they are dying tend to reflect on their past. This reflection can bear wonderful fruit. Now there is time to reconcile broken relationships, to die without resentment, to seek forgiveness and experience God's boundless mercy.

God forgives what the self-righteous and society will not forgive. Jesus walked among us to assure us of that. Even at the last hour of his life, when he was dying on the Cross, Jesus promised Paradise to a common criminal (Luke 23:43).

So put your heart at ease. Take comfort in the merciful Jesus of the Gospels and forgive yourself, because God has already forgiven you. And, of course, forgive those who have trespassed into your life. Leave this earth with a pure heart and you will surely see God.

Judge not, and you will not be judged; condemn not, and you will not be condemned; forgive, and you will be forgiven (Luke 6:37).

4. New Life Beyond Grief

Now if Christ is preached as raised from
the dead, how can some of you say that
there is no resurrection of the dead?
But if there is no resurrection of the
dead, then Christ has not been raised;
if Christ has not been raised, then our
preaching is in vain and your faith is
in vain . . . But in fact Christ has been
raised from the dead, the first fruits
of those who have fallen asleep.

1 Corinthians 15:12-14,20

Do Not Grieve Unduly

Love bears all things, believes all things, hopes all things, endures all things.

Grief is the price we pay for love. The greater our capacity for love, the greater our anguish when death separates us from seeing, hearing, and touching a person we love.

Once we surrender to love, we open ourselves to sacrificing for the beloved during his or her lifetime. We also open ourselves to suffering the pain of loss when the beloved dies. Yet, to paraphrase a famous line, "Isn't it better to have loved and suffered than never to have loved at all?"

When a loved one dies, be kind to yourself; don't allow yourself to be pressured by the artificial expectations of society. Losing the person you love is pain enough without punishing yourself with extra sacrifice and suffering.

Becoming a recluse is never a proof of love. After a time in mourning, it is important to start functioning again as a normal person, enjoying things that made you happy before the loss. Christian faith promises us unimaginable happiness in the afterlife. Open yourself fully to the knowledge that all is well with the person you love.

O give thanks to the LORD, for he is good;
his steadfast love endures for ever! (Psalm 118:1)

Surviving the Death of a Spouse

Brethren, . . . forgetting what lies behind and straining forward to what lies ahead, I press on toward the goal for the prize of the upward call of God in Christ Jesus.
                                                        Philippians 3:13-14

Grief results not only from the pain of loss but also from dependence on the person who has died. In regard to this dependence, we can do something to ease the pain: we can seek our own security and self-sufficiency.

In the first days of grief we feel helpless. We wonder how we can ever function again without the deceased. This is especially true when it is our spouse who has died.

Being dependent on a spouse is not a proof of love. And what we do not know when our spouse dies can definitely hurt us. There are countless stories about widows who knew nothing about domestic finances or how to take care of the car or how the boiler works. Equally helpless are widowers who have been nothing more than spectators to cooking, cleaning, and doing the wash.

Marriage entails shared responsibility and shared knowledge of how to survive. Even then it is difficult enough to start functioning normally again. The best investment for an easier grief is to have the knowledge and self-confidence that we can survive alone.

*God, grant me the serenity to accept
the things I cannot change,
the courage to change the things I can,
and the wisdom to know the difference.
(Prayer of St. Francis)*

Grief Has No Times

But we would not have you ignorant, brethren, concerning those who are asleep, that you may not grieve as others do who have no hope. For since we believe that Jesus died and rose again, even so, through Jesus, God will bring with him those who have fallen asleep.

1 Thessalonians 4:13-14

Grief is not the same thing as mourning and bereavement. Mourning is the period of ritual sorrow which custom and culture impose. Bereavement is the outer, visible expression of our inner pain. That inner pain — the anguish and emptiness — is what is meant by grief.

Mourning has specific time limits — seven days, thirty days, a year, or whatever custom expects. Even bereavement has a time limit. Society grants three days away from work. During this time the usual expressions of bereavement are accepted as normal. At the end of three days, however, it is back to work — business as usual.

When mourning and bereavement are over, grief continues for a lifetime. Our life is never quite the same again. As we live into the future, we inevitably experience "pangs" of grief. There is no time limit to grief.

Just when we least expect it, a favorite song or a travel brochure recalls a memory. An anniversary appears on the calendar, leaving us heartsick. If it happens to you, know that it is perfectly normal. You are simply experiencing the "pang" of grief which defies time and therapy.

May God be gracious to us and bless us
and make his face to shine upon us (Psalm 67:1).

Living with the Pain of Loss

So you have sorrow now, but I will see you again and your hearts will rejoice, and no one will take your joy from you.
John 16:22

At every new stage in life we experience loss. Going to kindergarten or into the military, for example, people experience the loss of loved ones. Marriage, menopause, and retirement are other examples. Every new step entails a breaking of ties — a loss.

As you handle such losses better, you are preparing yourself to handle the grief that comes with the loss of a loved one.

In any loss there is always pain. Do not take shortcuts or drugs to try to avoid the reality. For awhile you must live with the pain, waiting patiently for time to heal you.

Get as much rest as you need. Eat properly. Keep decision-making to a minimum. Stick to your normal schedule. Reaffirm your faith. Seek out the guidance of family and friends. Develop new interests. And anticipate happier days; their arrival is only a matter of time.

Why are you cast down, O my soul,
and why are you disquieted within me?
Hope in God; for I shall again praise him,
my help and my God . . . (Psalm 42:5-6).

Finding New Meaning

. . . I saw the Lord always before me, for he is at my right hand that I may not be shaken; therefore my heart was glad, and my tongue rejoiced; moreover my flesh will dwell in hope. For thou wilt not abandon my soul to Hades, nor let thy Holy One see corruption. Thou hast made known to me the ways of life; thou wilt make me full of gladness with thy presence.

Acts 2:25-28

Part of us dies when a loved one dies. We experience an emptiness in ourselves. If we are to resolve our grief, we must fill that emptiness with new meaning.

New meaning is found ahead of us, not in the past. As Viktor Frankl emphasizes so well in his classic book *Man's Search for Meaning,* we cannot go forward in life if we are constantly looking backward.

The grieving person has new projects to fulfill, new attachments to form, new dreams to live out. If we are truly faithful to the living spirit of the deceased, if we truly love them, we will continue our own journey to perfection without the chains of self-pity and pessimism.

The LORD is my shepherd . . . .
Even though I walk through the valley
of the shadow of death, I fear no evil;
for thou art with me;
thy rod and thy staff, they comfort me
(Psalm 23:1,4).

Support in the Midst of Grief

Let us then pursue what makes for peace and for mutual upbuilding.

Romans 14:19

In one of her songs, Barbra Streisand professes that the luckiest people in the world are those who need other people. When you are experiencing grief, you need people. You need their support and understanding.

In the midst of grief it is natural to withdraw into isolation. But don't let yourself become a recluse. Allow family and friends to draw you into their lives. Accept their hospitality and invitations.

In the early stage of grief, your main accomplishment is simply survival — going through the motions of normal functioning. As time passes, your awareness of the world around you increases. People astound you with their caring. When you arrive at that point, you have passed through the worst of your grief. You can look forward now to returning to your normal routine.

Blessed be the God and Father of our Lord
Jesus Christ, the Father of mercies and
God of all comfort, who comforts us in
all our affliction, so that we may
be able to comfort those who are in any
affliction . . . (2 Corinthians 1:3-4).

When a Child Dies

Your children are not your children
They come through you but not from you
And though they are with you
Yet they belong not to you
You may give them your love
You may house their bodies but not their souls
For their souls dwell in the house of tomorrow

Kahlil Gibran

The most painful of all grief comes from the death of a child. When our parents die we lose our past. When our spouse dies we lose our present. When a child of ours dies we lose our very future.

So many dreams are destroyed. We feel that death has cheated our child. We feel angry at our helplessness. And we feel guilt at the thought that maybe the child would still be alive if we had been more careful.

The death of a child can threaten the harmony of a marriage. Even in the midst of intense grief, the parents need to realize that accusations are much more a source of harm to their marriage than a source of relief from pain. Even though they may feel guilty about it, they need to return to the mutual sharing of things that give them pleasure and emotional satisfaction.

Out of the depths I cry to thee, O LORD!
LORD, hear my voice!
I wait for the LORD, my soul waits,
and in his word I hope . . . (Psalm 130:1,5).

The Yizkor Memorial Prayer

We shall not see the familiar glowing face, the warm, illuminated eyes nor hear the beloved voice.

We shall not sit face-to-face, across the family table or side by side in the home of a friend or in worship.

We shall not feel the kiss that once evoked our deepest response. *Yet death has failed.*

For the beloved who is gone lives and will always live through the years not in some distant corner of our being, to be uncovered only in a rare moment or by a sudden surge of recall.

The beloved has become a presence, indwelling and inseparable, rooted so deep that life cannot carry us far from the cherished center of memory and love.

Your hand, O Death, has been stayed. You cannot inflict oblivion or disappearance of those who were life of our life. They live and move within us, in spheres beyond your dominion.

We thank thee, O God of life and love, for the resurrecting gift of memory which endows thy children, fashioned in thy image, with Godlike sovereign power to give immortality through love. Blessed be thou, O God, who enable thy children to remember.

Teach us to live wisely and unselfishly in truth and understanding, in love and peace, so that those who come after us may likewise remember us for good, as we this day affectionately remember them who were unto us a blessing.

They live in us, in our hopes, and so shall their influence continue in our children. In thee, O Lord, they and we are one.

Communing with Loved Ones

Now he is not God of the dead, but of the living; for all live to him.

Luke 20:38

Do we need our bodies to communicate with one another? Can people be in contact mentally without using their bodily senses? Many people can remember getting a phone call from someone they were just thinking about. When this happens, is it always mere coincidence? Could it be that, sometimes at least, people are in contact spiritually before they communicate vocally?

If it is true that we can experience a living person's thoughts or state of mind, why would it not be equally possible to be in telepathic contact with someone who is deceased?

If you should ever sense the presence of, or a message from, a dear one who has died, do not consider it odd. Studies have shown that such experiences are not at all uncommon. They are very common.

Likewise, do not consider yourself abnormal when you communicate ideas or sentiments to a deceased loved one.

People pray, confident that they are heard, to Jesus and to well-known saints. Why should we not communicate with equal confidence to our deceased father, mother, spouse, or child? Be in touch with those you love. Death is no barrier to communication; to God all are alive.

> *I shall not die, but I shall live,*
> *and recount the deeds*
> *of the LORD (Psalm 118:17).*

Letting Go

Our God is a God of salvation;
and to GOD, the Lord, belongs escape from
death.

Psalm 68:20

Death has been described as an oxymoron — a combination of opposites. On the one hand, death is very final. The body of the deceased person deteriorates and we experience it as lifeless. On the other hand, life goes on. The person's spirit not only survives but enjoys a whole new freedom of expression.

Despite the sadness of farewell, Christian faith calls us to celebrate the new life into which the loved one has entered. As lovers of the deceased and as Christians, we want our loved one to have the freedom and joy of afterlife. We willingly "let go."

This process of "letting go" is important — for us. It helps us to return to normal from our grief.

My soul thirsts for God, for the living God.
Oh send out thy light and thy truth;
let them lead me . . . (Psalm 42:2, 43:3).

5. Live Life to the Full

Put off your old nature which belongs
to your former manner of life and is
corrupt through deceitful lusts, and
be renewed in the spirit of your minds,
and put on the new nature, created
after the likeness of God in true
righteousness and holiness.

Ephesians 4:22-24

Praise While There Is Time

Do not save your loving speeches for your friends until they are dead. Do not write them on their tombstones, speak them now instead.

Anna Cummins

The word *eulogy* means "compliment." Unfortunately, the word has been relegated to the funeral rite because it is not customary to praise people when they are alive.

One of the components of grief is a sense of guilt. In many instances this sense of guilt flows from our failure to tell people, while they are still alive, how much they mean to us. The honest praise we give to another returns to console us after the person has died.

If you want to be more sensitive to the good in others, think of your own mortality. The fact that you will not be here forever can move you to focus on others' outstanding qualities rather than their minor flaws.

See that none of you repays evil for evil,
but always seek to do good to one another
and to all (1 Thessalonians 5:15).

Look at Death, Live Life

As each has received a gift, employ it for one another, as good stewards of God's varied grace.

1 Peter 4:10

The best way to relieve our fear of dying and death is to enjoy a full life. As Herman Feifel suggests, "To think about death when one is not sure of the meaning of life is bound to be upsetting."

Dr. Elisabeth Kubler-Ross shares a similar reflection: "This is perhaps the greatest lesson I have learned from my patients: Live, so you do not have to look back and say, 'God, how I have wasted my life!' "

Confronting your mortality each day is far from morbid. In fact, it gives you an urgency about time which eliminates waste, depression, arguments, and procrastination. It invites a fullness of love, a search for deeper meaning, and a desire to influence your milieu in a positive way.

Confronting your mortality keeps you from drifting into the stream of those who have no sense of purpose. It helps you to see your loved one, your work, and your worries in a much clearer light.

Teach us, O Lord, not to neglect the task of today because we cannot see its eternal effect. Teach us to number our days that we may apply our hearts to wisdom, to lengthen our brief life by intensity of living and to fill swift hours with worthy deeds. (Hebrew Meditation)

You Can't Take It with You

Do not deprive yourself of a happy day;
let not your share of desired good pass by you.
Will you not leave the fruit of your labours to another,
and what you acquired by toil to be divided by lot?
                                        Sirach 14:14-15

Confronting your mortality can keep you from being a stingy, chronic saver who gives up nice experiences in life because of greed. Put your interest in life, not in the bank.

The word *satisfaction* comes from the Latin *satis* (enough) *facere* (to make). Some people are never satisfied because they do not realize when they have made enough money for their needs. Do not spend so much time making money that you have little time to enjoy its fruits.

Of course, be financially responsible. Plan for the future. But don't let the pursuit of money become a cancer that kills what is most important in life. Don't wait for cardiac arrest or terminal illness to remind you of the old adage: "You can't take it with you."

This is the day which the LORD has made;
let us rejoice and be glad in it (Psalm 118:24).

No Time for Pettiness

Do not give yourself over to sorrow,
and do not afflict yourself deliberately.
Gladness of heart is the life of man,
and the rejoicing of a man is length of days.

Sirach 30:21-22

Confronting your mortality has great dividends for relieving anxiety and depression. Once you realize that life is so short, you are willing to take risks to relieve your frustration, willing to simplify your life-style, willing to adjust your behavior so as to ease your anxiety.

Confronting your mortality can also enlighten you to the absurdity of resentment and revenge. Pettiness and foolish arguments make life unhappy. When you realize the brevity of your life-span, you have no time for such negative things.

Grief is hard enough to resolve without complicating the heartache with guilt. It is pure anguish to say good-bye and whisper "I am sorry" and "I love you," wishing you had said it long before.

A cheerful heart is a good medicine,
but a downcast spirit dries up the bones
(Proverbs 17:22).

The Diary of Your Life

The pessimist resembles the person who observes with fear and sadness that the wall calendar, from which he daily tears a sheet, grows thinner with each passing day. On the other hand, the person who ventures into each day removes each successive leaf and files it away with a few diary notes. He can reflect with pride and joy about the richness of a full life.

Viktor Frankl

The "diary" of our life is the one book we all write. Usually our story has chapters of great joy and sadness, of delight and disillusionment. Hopefully, it has a happy ending.

The best gift you can leave for your family and friends when you die is the memory of a life well spent, a life of giving and caring.

If the life story you are writing is not as good as you would like, consider writing some new chapters. The last pages are best remembered. Even old Scrooge, in Dickens' Christmas story, changed his life at the thought of death. Make your life a Merry Christmas and you will not have to worry about a Happy Easter.

. . . that I may know him and the power of
his resurrection, and may share his sufferings,
becoming like him in his death . . . (Philippians 3:10).

The Rule of Forgiveness

For if you forgive men their trespasses, your heavenly Father also will forgive you; but if you do not forgive men their trespasses, neither will your Father forgive your trespasses.

Matthew 6:14-15

Jesus had great love and mercy for sinners, but hard judgments for hypocrites. You will receive God's mercy if you have forgiven others their faults and reconciled yourself with the people you have hurt with hypocritical judgments and criticism.

There are some self-righteous people who will have a rude awakening when they die. If they expect from God what they refuse to others, they are deluding themselves. Before you ask forgiveness from God, reconcile yourself with anyone you have hurt, anyone you refuse to forgive.

And forgive us our debts,
   As we also have forgiven our debtors . . .
(Matthew 6:12).

Do Not Save the Cake

. . . I will not be a burden, for I seek not what is yours but you . . . I will most gladly spend and be spent for your souls.

2 Corinthians 12:14,15)

The story is told of Mike who was breathing his last day of human life. His wife Bridget tried to restrain her grief by busying herself in the kitchen.

Bridget baked and frosted a lovely chocolate cake that filled the whole house with its aroma. When she finished, she looked in on poor Mike and asked if he wanted anything.

Mike licked his dry lips and asked for nothing but a small slice of that lovely chocolate cake which filled his nostrils with such a sweet scent. "Not on your life," barked Bridget, "that cake is for your wake."

Confronting your mortality should direct your attention to your family. These individuals have been handpicked by God as the special people in your life. They are your first priority. If you are going to be generous and caring, let it be with them.

Some people spend so much time crusading for family values that their own families are falling apart. Do not save the cake for the wake. Care now for the people God has entrusted to you.

Teach us, O Lord, not to neglect the task of today because we cannot see its eternal effect. (Hebrew Meditation)

The Aura of the Soul?

So is it with the resurrection of the dead. What is sown is perishable, what is raised is imperishable. It is sown in dishonour, it is raised in glory. It is sown in weakness, it is raised in power.

1 Corinthians 15:42-43

For centuries artists have painted Jesus, Saint Francis, and other holy persons with halos or auras above their heads.

In recent years a new development called Kirlian photography shows on film what looks like an aura surrounding people's bodies. In his book *Afterlife: The Other Side of Death,* Morton Kelsey remarks: "The Kirlian process has shown that these auras vary in width of the flares, as well as in color and intensity, according to the person's mental and physical condition. It is interesting that the places where the strongest flares are observed correspond directly to the points on Chinese acupuncture charts."

Does Kirlian photography show us the "spiritual body" that Saint Paul speaks of in 1 Corinthians? The two may have no connection at all. But we can say this: people who draw halos and people who speak of a nonphysical body are not necessarily crackpots. As Morton Kelsey observes, "The soul seems to have some observable effects."

Eternal rest grant unto them, O Lord,
and let perpetual light shine upon them.
(Prayer for the Dead)

Do Not Put Off Living

Do not say to your neighbour, "Go, and come again,
tomorrow I will give it" — when you have it with you.
                                                    Proverbs 3:28

Lucifer was seeking a way to subvert humankind. The devil who came up with the most promising plan would be sent to earth. Three devils accepted the challenge.

"Send me," the first devil said. "I will tell people there is no God." Lucifer replied: "The human being may be weak and foolish but he is not entirely stupid. He cannot deny the evidence of the universe around him. He knows there has to be a Cause for all creation. This plan could fool only a very few."

"Send me," said the second devil. "I will tell people there is no hell." Lucifer replied: "That is better, but still not good enough. Even those who believe you will be afraid there just might be a hell."

"Send me," said the third devil. "I will tell people that there is no hurry to be good. They can wait until they get old." The third devil got the job and has been wreaking havoc on earth ever since.

Do not wait for your first retirement check to enjoy life and people and nature. Death can be frightening for the person who waits too long and then realizes that death is going to take it away, just as he is really beginning to enjoy life.

Lord, help us not to put off till tomorrow
the good we can do or enjoy today. (Ancient Saying)

Contemplate Life

As you are now
So once was I.
As I am now
Soon you will be.

Tombstone Epitaph

In the August 1970 issue of *Psychology Today,* Edwin Shneidman conducted a survey entitled "You and Death." More than 30,000 readers responded, which broke *Psychology Today's* previous response record of 20,000 set by a sex questionnaire.

In the "You and Death" survey people were asked what was the most significant factor that formed their attitude. The majority responded with words such as *introspection* and *personal meditation.* This small booklet, it is hoped, helps you to engage in that kind of meditation. Answers to your personal questions about dying and death are waiting to be discovered within you.

Writing this booklet has given me a special sense of intimacy with the living spirit of my dad, more awareness of my purpose in life, and more love for my family and friends. Let me suggest that you start writing down your own reflections. Death is more on your mind than you think. Confront your hopes and fears. Follow the journey of your soul, homeward bound.

OTHER HELPFUL PUBLICATIONS FROM LIGUORI THAT OFFER COMFORT AND COURAGE

HOW TO FACE DEATH WITHOUT FEAR
adapted from the writings of St. Alphonsus
by Norman J. Muckerman, C.SS.R.

A series of deeply spiritual reflections by the Doctor of Prayer, St. Alphonsus, who tells you how to live so you are always ready to die. Offers commonsense attitudes on the mystery of death, together with reasons and motives for facing death with courage and with confidence in a merciful and forgiving Father. $1.50

COPING WITH WIDOWHOOD
by Frances Caldwell Durland

This is a book of sadness yet of joy, of groping, and of healing. In it, a widow tells her own story of how she learned to "cope" with the pain, the shock, the bewilderment of losing a mate, a life's partner. To her, coping did not mean just "getting along." It meant growing through suffering to find again the richness, fullness, and beauty of LIFE — even if it meant a life alone. $1.50

HOW TO PRAY WHEN TROUBLED
From His Cross to Yours
by Andrew Costello, C.SS.R.

Encourages meditation on the Seven Last Words of Jesus, shows how we can pray in the same words when we face suffering and pain. $1.50

HOW TO TELL YOUR CHILD ABOUT DEATH
by Patrick Kaler, C.SS.R.

Suggests specific ideas and situations to use in presenting the concept of death — both its finality and the Christian message that death is not only an end but a beginning. 35¢

COMFORT FOR THOSE IN MOURNING
by D. F. Moran, C.SS.R.

Points out the spiritual value in mourning and discusses the truths about death that God has revealed to us through our Christian faith. 35¢